MAIR

Weegie Wan-Liners

MAIR
Weegie Wan-Liners

Ian Black

BLACK & WHITE PUBLISHING

First published 2013
by Black & White Publishing Ltd
29 Ocean Drive, Edinburgh EH6 6JL

1 3 5 7 9 10 8 6 4 2   13 14 15 16

ISBN   978 1 84502 702 5

A CIP catalogue record for this book is available
from the British Library.

Typeset by RefineCatch Limited, Bungay
Printed and bound in Poland
www.hussarbooks.pl

Introduction

Here it is, due to popular demand (honest!), the second book of Weegie Wan-Liners, designed for the discerning denizens of our fair city. And for total nut jobs as well, of course. We are the people who say to our husbands and wives: 'Naw, they troosers don't make ye look any fatter. How could they?' We also say things like: 'You're a bit of a babe, you ur. Huv ye seen the movie?' And: 'Hur face is hur chaperone', bad bastards that we are, but we are mostly trying to be funny. Sometimes.

Sometimes we aren't, though, and this compendium of carping and coarse calling might serve as ammunition in the pub turf wars and the blagging that often serves as social intercourse in Glasgow. If you are the kind of person who feels free to say: 'Whit has a toty brain, a big mooth, and an opinion nobody gives a rat's erse aboot? You!' then welcome home, sister or brother, this is the very book for you.

If you have ever wanted to describe someone as: 'A parasite for sore eyes', or have wished to say: 'Listen pal, you ur so borin people fa' asleep haufwey through yer name', but couldn't find the words, and/or the courage, then get wired right into this, it will help.

But ca' canny. Remember where you are. Stay light on your feet. Look both ways before you cross someone (or the road), and as Dixon of Dock Green (people under sixty, ask your granny) used to say: 'Mind how you go.'

Weegie Questions

Is that yer real face
or are ye still oot fur
yer Halloween?

How many times dae
Ah huv tae flush ye before
ye go away?

What are ye going to be IF ye grow up?

Oh good Christ, look
at you. Anybuddy else
hurt in the accident?

Did you eat a brain tumour for breakfast?

When ye go to the
mind reader wumman,
dae ye get hauf price?

Kin Ah get in the
queue tae hate you?

Weegie Threats
and Insults

A' yer learnin curves
look like Mount Everest,
tae you, don't they?

Naw, they troosers don't
make ye look fatter.
How could they?

Wherr's yer girlfriend?
Ootside grazin, Ah suppose.

Whit has a toty brain,
a big mooth and an
opinion naebuddy gives
a rat's erse aboot?
You!

Yer bus leaves in 10 minutes.
Be under it.

Ahm no quite gettin
whit yer sayin. Ahm
wearin ma moron filter.

Listen, pal. Thank fuck Ahm
no as stupit as you look.

Naebuddy likes Jimmy at furst sight. It saves time.

Lookin at your face is like readin in the motor. It's a' right for five minutes, then ye start tae feel sick.

Big John here?
He thinks bipolar is a
sexually mixed-up bear.

Wullie has a one-way ticket on the Disoriented Express.

Talkin tae you is difficult.
Ah don't speak alcoholic.

You've goat jist the right
kind ae looks fur the movies.
Two mair legs and ye could
be in a Western.

Davie, good tae see ye again,
back in men's clothing.

He's really intae himself.
His heid is up his arse.

Were Jimmy's parents related? Well, they did huv the same last name.

Wullie there, he's wan ae
nine. His folks urny bead
rattlers or that, thur jist
reckless.

John's goat an inferiority complex, but no a very good wan.

He's goat a nose like a
trigonometry problem.

He has double chins a'
the wey doon tae his belly.

He's goat a winning smile,
but everythin else is a loser.

His face is full ae
broken commandments.

Billy here is differently clued.
Disny know much, but he's tap
ae the league in nose hair.

He has the attention span
ae a streak o' lightning.

His golf bag disny contain
a full set ae irons.

Aye, Bill is an auld hippie.
Seen it all, done it all, canny
remember most ae it.

Ye look intae his eyes,
an ye get the feelin
somebuddy else is drivin.

Failure has gone tae his heid.

Even the grave yawns fur him.

Tangerine here? He's that
narra mindit that if he fell
on a pin it would blind him
in baith eyes.

Naebuddy kin huv a higher opinion of him than Ah have; and Ah think he's a prick.

Listen, pal, you ur so borin
people fa' asleep haufwey
through yer name.

He's aboot as useful
as a fitba' bat.

He's a gross ignoramus.
144 times worse than yer
average ignoramus.

You ur a parasite
for sore eyes.

Ye sound reasonable. It must be time fur another drink.

He's a wee thing too tall
for his blood supply.

The only culture you've
goat is the bacteria in
yer belly, ya pranny.

Please don't breed,
crater-face.

Aye, he uses his heid,
but it's mainly tae keep
the rain oot ae his neck.

Everybuddy has a right tae be ugly, but that yin is abusin the privilege.

She niffs like an
alkie's cairpet.

She's goat a face like she's
been ram-raidin oan a scooter.

You've goat a loat of pride,
but no much tae be proud of.

Torn face, you ur a
haemorrhoid on the
arse of the world.

He's only a legend in his
ain mind, a bliddy minefield
ae misinformation.

Donny, yer a medical mystery.
A waste ae skin.

He's a mental midget wi the
IQ of a wee toty chucky stane.

She's aboot as useful as a
sleepin pill oan a honeymoon.

You've goat a Neanderthal brain in a Cro-Magnon body. Scary, and no in a good wey.

You ur a mental pacifist oot ae necessity. Yer always gonny lose in a battle ae wits.

You ur a peripheral
visionary, so ye ur.

Ye claim that you've goat
a photographic memory,
but therr's nae film, and
the lens cover seems tae
be glued oan.

You ur a poor excuse for protoplasm, an a prime candidate for natural deselection.

Yer a real rocket scientologist,
wi a room temperature IQ.
That's centigrade, by the way.

Ye might huv a titanic
intellect, son, but this world
is full ae icebergs.

It's kind of like you've
goat a vacuum-tube brain
in a microchip world.

Ye should be the subject
ae retroactive birth control.
Yer a walkin argument for
post-natal abortion.

Yer brain's like a wind-up
clock wi nae key.

Ye kept a' yer eggs in
the wan basket, didn't ye?
An then ye drapt it.

Ah blame aliens. They've zapped ye with a stupidity ray . . . merr than wance.

Listen, boy, you ur alive today only because it's illegal to kill ye.

A' he remembers about his
middle name is the first letter.

Every time Ah look at ye
Ahm already visualising the
duct tape ower yer mooth.

Always in the right place,
but at the wrang time.

You, away hame an sharpen
up yer sleeping skills.

Always speaks her mind,
Mary, so usually she's
speechless.

Tommy's goat an ego
like a black hole.

Sean is an example of
how the dinosaurs survived
for millions ae years wi
walnut-sized brains.

Jimmy is an experiment in artificial stupidity.

Ony slower and
he'd be in reverse.

If Graeme wis ony smarter
he'd be an eejit.

Yon yin? Argues wi
hersel – and loses.

Yer entire life you've been aboot as focused as a fart.

Attic's a wee bit dusty,
and spring cleanin's
no gonny help.

Weegie Philosophy

Ony connection between his reality and oors is pure coincidental. And ony similarity between him and a human being is the same.

Billy, ye suffer from whit
Ah call ano-fossal ambiguity.
Ye canny tell yer erse fae
a hole in the grun.

Calum's a 20th-century man.
Nae future.

Look, we a' huv somethin
tae bring tae this discussion.
But Ah think from noo oan
the thing you should bring
is silence.

Some folk ur wise and
some ur otherwise.

Yer heid is like a squerr
with only three sides.

A standard deviant, you ur, a statue in a world of pigeons.

She's like a teapot
with a cracked lid.

Iain can easily be
confused by facts.

Weegie Insults
to Men

He mebbe looks like an
eejit and sounds like an eejit,
but don't let that confuse
ye . . . he really is an eejit.

Romance? Ma Eddie?
His idea ae romance is
openin his can ae Tennent's
away fae ma face.

Jim here was never a'
that comfortable eating wi
ma family – we yase
knives and forks.

I widny want to put him
in charge ae snake
control in Ireland.

Gaun ya hamshank,
yer baws are a' beef.

Young Boaby? Canny count
his balls and get the same
answer twice. He couldny
count tae 21 if he hud bare
feet and wis in the scuddy.

Big Jim couldny get laid if he crawled up a chicken's erse and waited his turn.

Davie's the same.
Couldny get a shag in
a monkey whorehouse
wi a bag ae bananas.

Him? Aw foam, nae beer.

He's goat wan ae they faces that looks as if it wis designed in a wind tunnel.

Jock claims tae be better
at sex than anybuddy; noo
aw he needs is a partner.

He wis born too late –
he'd have been a great
Neanderthal.

Stupit? Yon yin couldny hit sand if he fell aff a camel. In fact he wid be unlikely tae hit watter if he fell aff a boat.

John is aboot as bright as a
bulb . . . a daffodil bulb.

At least he hus a
positive attitude aboot
his destructive habits.

He's aboot as useful as
a carpet fitter's ladder.

He's goat an intellect
matched only by garden tools.
Wee toty tiny garden tools.

He's aboot as sensible as entering an erse-kickin contest wi a porcupine.

Peter's goat a brain kinda like wet trainies. It makes squishy noises when runnin.

Yer a kinda modest wee guy, Pat, wi quite a loat tae be modest aboot.

Davie wid huv tae gie
up chewing gum jist
tae look stupit.

Weegie Insults
to Women

Hur, she's goat a face like a rerr Chinese vase – mingin.

She's seen merr coke
than a bottle of Bacardi.

Don't look oot ae the
windae. People will
think it's Halloween.

That yin, when she entered an ugly contest, they said, 'Sorry, nae professionals.'

Hur, when she looks oot the windae she gets arrested fur moonin.

She's that ugly they
filmed *Gorillas in the Mist*
in hur shower.

She's that ugly even Rice
Krispies won't talk tae hur.

She's that ugly that people go oot as hur for Halloween.

Harry's wife's that ugly
that he takes her tae work
with him so that he disny
huv tae kiss her goodbye.

She must have hud a
magnificent body before
hur belly went in for a
career o' its ain.

She's that pure even Moses couldny part hur knees.

She wis born ugly,
and built to last.

She cackles a lot, but Ah huvny seen any eggs yet.

Hur face is hur chaperone.

Oh aye, no bad lookin,
but you couldny find her
IQ with a searchlight.

The finest woman that ever walked the streets.

An you, Senga, huv a' the sex
appeal ae a wet paper poke
fulla boak. Pit them away!

Knackered? She's as worn oot as a cucumber in a convent.

Mary answers the door
when the phone rings.

She's feart she'll cancel
hur guarantee if she thinks
too much.

She is a wumman of rerr
intelligence. It's rerr when
she shows any.